FANTASTIC
BEASTS
AND WHERE
TO FIND THEM

NEWT
SCAMANDER

A MOVIE SCRAPBOOK

CANDLEWICK
PRESS

An Insight Editions Book

Newt Scamander

New Friendships

Porpentina "Tina" Goldstein

Queenie Goldstein

Jacob Kowalski

— ✦ ✹ ✧ —

New York City

New York City, 1926

A City in Turmoil

New Salem Philanthropic Society

Other Spots

Urban Life and Magic

Fantastic Items

— ✦ ✹ ✧ —

Creatures

Creating Fantastic Beasts

Beastly Beginnings

Newt's Case

What's Next?

— ✦ ✹ ✧ —

Newt Scamander is the foremost expert on magical beasts in J.K. Rowling's Wizarding World. His classic Magizoology textbook, *Fantastic Beasts and Where to Find Them*, is required reading for students at schools of witchcraft and wizardry such as Hogwarts.

The *Fantastic Beasts and Where to Find Them* film explores Newt's life before he finished writing his classic book and became a household name. J.K. Rowling's screenplay brings us back to 1926, a time when a young Newt first arrived in New York City on a mission concerning a rare magical creature. Newt's arrival with a case full of creatures almost immediately presents a challenge for a wizarding community trying hard to remain a secret.

The real-world task of creating Newt's creatures and the 1920s wizarding world was just as challenging. Filmmakers, actors, costume designers, and many more all came together to bring the story to life. This movie scrapbook—chock-full of unique keepsakes and artifacts—offers a behind-the-scenes look at Newt Scamander, his creatures, his friends, and his world, as they were imagined for the movie.

Through art, sketches, diagrams, maps, and more, the magic of Newt's world from the film is yours to adventure through!

Newt Scamander

Before he became the wizarding world's most famous Magizoologist, Newt Scamander attended Hogwarts, where he was a Hufflepuff. Though Newt was expelled from the school, actor Eddie Redmayne knew that in representing Newt he wasn't playing the part of an average troublemaker. Newt's natural curiosity and love of his creatures set him apart. "I like Newt's wonder. I like the way that he takes things as he sees them," says Eddie.

As a Magizoologist, Newt often travels alone to remote parts of the world. Eddie kept this in mind while playing the character, especially when Newt first arrives in New York City. "I think New York even now is the most frenzied, wonderful, noisy, and colorful of places," explains Eddie. "For Newt, having spent a year by himself and suddenly stepping into this city, I think there's definitely a wonder there and a curiosity about everything around him."

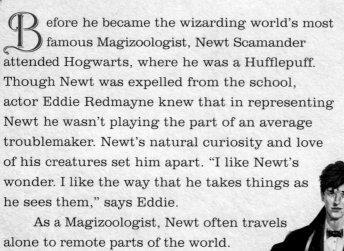

THE CASE

Newt carries an enchanted case full of creatures he has found on his travels, and he is completely devoted to caring for them and keeping them safe. As Eddie explains it, "Newt cares passionately about magical creatures. He'll go anywhere in the world to find them. And he'll do anything to protect them. In a way, he knows his beasts better than he knows himself. He certainly understands beasts better than he does people!"

New Friendships

PORPENTINA "TINA" GOLDSTEIN

Formerly an Auror at MACUSA, Tina was demoted to the lowly position of clerk in the Wand Permit Office with her sister, Queenie. She spots Newt at a New Salem Philanthropic Society rally on the steps of the Steen National Bank and senses he's up to something.

But Newt and Tina share certain similarities—both in terms of their passion for their work and their outsider status—and a kinship develops between the two. "She knows she has a lot of potential, but she can't seem to express it and convince people of it. Newt sees all that potential in her," recalls actress Katherine Waterston. "I think that's a lot of what falling in love is. You feel someone else recognizing what you are, what you have to offer."

Tina Goldstein's MACUSA identification card and Admonitor bracelet

M.A.C.U.S.A
IDENTIFICATION

As in most of J.K. Rowling's work, the central story in her *Fantastic Beasts and Where to Find Them* screenplay revolves around a crew of unlikely companions who persevere through dark, difficult trials and end up as loyal friends.

QUEENIE GOLDSTEIN

Tina's younger sister, Queenie, literally gets into the head of most everyone she meets—she can read minds. She's glamorous and fun, but also very empathic. Best of all, Queenie has a big heart. She has a soft spot right away for Jacob.

For actress Alison Sudol, the best part about playing Queenie was, well, everything! "She's really fun and playful and perceptive," recalls Alison. "I find her very aware, but also unaware of herself when she's falling in love. She's also thrilled to be on an adventure. Everything that would scare most people is sort of thrilling for her."

✳ Fantastic Facts ✳

Flapper fashions are definitely one of the most iconic features of the 1920s, and Queenie dresses the part in the film. The costume designer created Queenie's look to reflect her carefree and fun personality, inspired by real flappers of that era.

JACOB KOWALSKI

One of Jacob's
beast-shaped pastries

J acob works at a canning factory, but his dream is to open a bakery that serves Polish baked goods. He meets Newt in the bank, and an unfortunate case swap follows. A veteran of World War I, he has seen and survived terrible things. So when the going gets tough for Newt, Jacob emerges as a strong and loyal friend.

As a No-Maj, Jacob may not possess any magical abilities, but he has other talents. "He loves cooking and baking for people," explains actor Dan Fogler. "He may not be able to perform magic, but he can make a little pastry that will knock your socks off."

Like many of the other characters, Jacob has potential that others struggle to see. His kind nature catches Queenie's eye. "He's a very loveable guy," continues Dan. "Jacob just loves making people happy."

NEW YORK CITY

NEW YORK CITY, 1926 ✳

The noisy and colorful place that Newt encounters in *Fantastic Beasts and Where to Find Them* is 1920s New York, so the filmmakers had to create a version of the city during that time. But, of course, it needed a magical twist. To build a city with a secret world full of witches and wizards, the magic had to fit in side by side with the New York that "No-Maj" history remembers.

The team started by doing their homework—clothes, buildings, and objects from the 1920s were studied carefully and then given a wizarding world spin.

Fantastic Facts

What is a No-Maj? Pronounced "no-madge," the word is slang for people without magical powers. It's the American version of the British word Muggle.

Speakeasy Culture

In the 1920s, the city's music scene was alive with a new energy. Lively jazz and dance tunes throbbed in New York's famous nightclubs—in fact, the 1920s are often referred to as the Jazz Age. Due to Prohibition laws, alcohol was illegal, which led to the creation of underground "speakeasy" clubs. In the film, Newt visits a magical speakeasy called The Blind Pig. Filmmakers used real-world secret clubs from that time as inspiration.

✴ Fantastic Facts ✴

Ron Perlman, who plays Gnarlak, the goblin owner of The Blind Pig, is quite a bit taller than his character. The filmmakers had to use several different scale techniques to create the illusion of a small but very powerful figure. First, a scaled-up version of The Blind Pig was constructed, with large tables and chairs. Then the other actors were given wooden blocks to stand or sit on so that they looked bigger than Ron when they interacted—as if he were just four feet tall! Ron's performance on set was then filmed through motion capture. Finally, that performance was digitally placed onto the computer-generated Gnarlak and combined into the live-action.

The Roaring Twenties

By the mid-1920s, the world was finally emerging from the shadow of the terrible war of the previous decade. New York had become a thriving, vibrant city of six million people. The new decade seemed full of promise. The increased availability of electricity made some exciting inventions more common—electric lights, telephones, radios, motion pictures. Automobiles roamed the city's newly paved streets. Airplanes crossed the oceans. Everything seemed new; anything seemed possible.

STRAND
BETTE DAVIS
in
MARKED WOMAN
with
HUMPHREY BOGART

SQUIBBS
DENTAL
CREAM

Concept art of the MACUSA lobby. MACUSA stands for Magical Congress of the United States of America.

The Art Deco Look

Art deco is a design style that was very popular in the 1920s and can be found in many New York City structures from that time period. The *Fantastic Beasts and Where to Find Them* team studied locations like the Chrysler Building, Rockefeller Center, and the interior of Radio City Music Hall when creating the world seen in the movie.

You can see the influence of art deco style on lots of things within the film, especially the entryway to MACUSA, the American version of the Ministry of Magic. Newt first visits MACUSA thanks to an American witch named Tina Goldstein, who tries to keep Newt's escaped creatures from exposing the wizarding community. The MACUSA headquarters are located in the Woolworth Building, a real place that still exists today and is located at 233 Broadway. In 1926, it was the tallest building in the world.

A City in Turmoil

The Salem Witch Trials of the 1690s marked one of the most significant witchcraft-related moments in American history. It's fitting that the MACUSA lobby would feature a striking memorial to the people who lost their lives during that time. For the monument depicting three women, a man, and a child, sculptor Bryn Court made a miniature clay version before creating the final full-scale versions, which were painted bronze.

In *Fantastic Beasts and Where to Find Them*, the persecution that distinguished the original Salem Witch Trials still exists in 1920s New York, as Newt learns almost immediately upon his arrival.

The MACUSA lobby, with its forty-foot golden phoenix statues up above and the Salem memorial on the floor

××× ISSUED BY THE MACUSA SURVEILLANCE DEPARTMENT ×××

ALWAYS BE VIGILANT

MACUSA MEMO

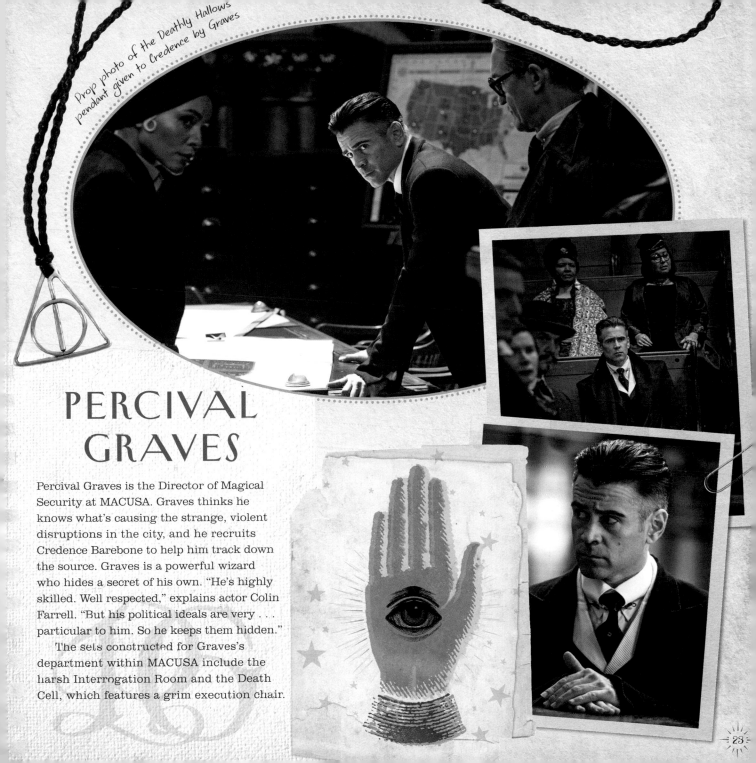

PERCIVAL GRAVES

Percival Graves is the Director of Magical Security at MACUSA. Graves thinks he knows what's causing the strange, violent disruptions in the city, and he recruits Credence Barebone to help him track down the source. Graves is a powerful wizard who hides a secret of his own. "He's highly skilled. Well respected," explains actor Colin Farrell. "But his political ideals are very . . . particular to him. So he keeps them hidden."

The sets constructed for Graves's department within MACUSA include the harsh Interrogation Room and the Death Cell, which features a grim execution chair.

NEW SALEM PHILANTHROPIC SOCIETY

Newt stumbles upon a rally held by the New Salem Philanthropic Society, an anti-magic group seeking to bring about another Salem-style witch hunt. The film's design team created N.S.P.S. propaganda leaflets for the scene that display the group's dangerous message.

HEED MY WORDS

CREDENCE BAREBONE

Growing up in the restrictive and abusive home of Mary Lou Barebone, Credence suppresses his natural abilities with disastrous results. Actor Ezra Miller understood the serious lessons represented by Credence's struggle: "It's important to explore the idea that there is cause and effect in the world, and the idea that someone who endures trauma has tough choices to make about how that trauma is going to affect the rest of their life. Whether that wound will be a blessing or a curse—I think it's a really potent subject."

MARY LOU BAREBONE

Mary Lou is the stern leader of the N.S.P.S. Played by Samantha Morton, she lives in an abandoned church with her three adopted children, Credence, Modesty, and Chastity. Mary Lou's somber costumes reflect her character's puritanical traits and stand in stark contrast to the elaborate and colorful costumes often seen in the wizarding world.

RS

Tues. ...S PM — Wed. 6.15 PM - Sunday 1 to 6 PM

✦ A Barebone Existence ✦

To create the Barebone home—which also serves as the N.S.P.S. headquarters—the team stuck to a sparse style. The home's plain interior was decorated with reminders of the society's harsher puritanical beliefs, such as creepy dolls and an A-to-Z Alphabet of Sin embroidery in Modesty's room.

Concept art for the old N.S.P.S. church and a photo of Chastity at the church entrance as seen in the film

OTHER SPOTS

Port Authority

The movie opens with Newt's arrival at the Port Authority Customhouse. Before filmmakers create a location, they imagine what it will look like through the use of illustrations called concept art. In this piece of concept art, you can see how they imagined the customs checkpoint where Newt presents his passport and hands over his case for inspection. Of course, Newt makes sure to set the case to "Muggle Worthy" first!

Steen National Bank

Steen National Bank is where Newt Scamander first meets Jacob Kowalski, who is played by Dan Fogler. As a No-Maj, Jacob is definitely shocked to encounter the wizarding world for the first time after Newt's mischievous creature, the Niffler, wreaks havoc on the bank while on the hunt for shiny treasures. "Jacob's not used to this sort of thing," says Dan, laughing. "He gets very disoriented whenever it happens!"

H. Teucher Jeweler

Newt and Jacob track Newt's Niffler to this glittering jewelry store.

URBAN LIFE AND MAGIC

To make Newt's world seem even more real, the graphics team created everything from magazines to posters. These items give us a sense of what life was like for a wizard or witch at that time.

What Do Witches and Wizards Read?

One good way to understand a community's everyday concerns is to glance through its newspapers and magazines. This is true for understanding wizards and witches, too. Do you want to scan the local news? Catch the Quidditch World Cup scores? Keep current with the latest bewitching fashions? Maybe you just "feel out of touch with your broom"? Thanks to the artists and designers working behind the scenes on the film, there is a publication for every wizardly interest. Here are just a few of the amazing periodicals and book covers created for *Fantastic Beasts* and *Where to Find Them*.

The specter of World War I lurks in the background of *Fantastic Beasts and Where to Find Them*, just as it did in the real 1920s. In the film, we learn that Jacob and Newt are both veterans of the war.

Wands

Wands are one of the most important props in any any movie about the wizarding world. Wandmaking is an art form, and every wand has to feel unique to its owner. Here's a look at the wands of the major magical characters in *Fantastic Beasts and Where to Find Them*.

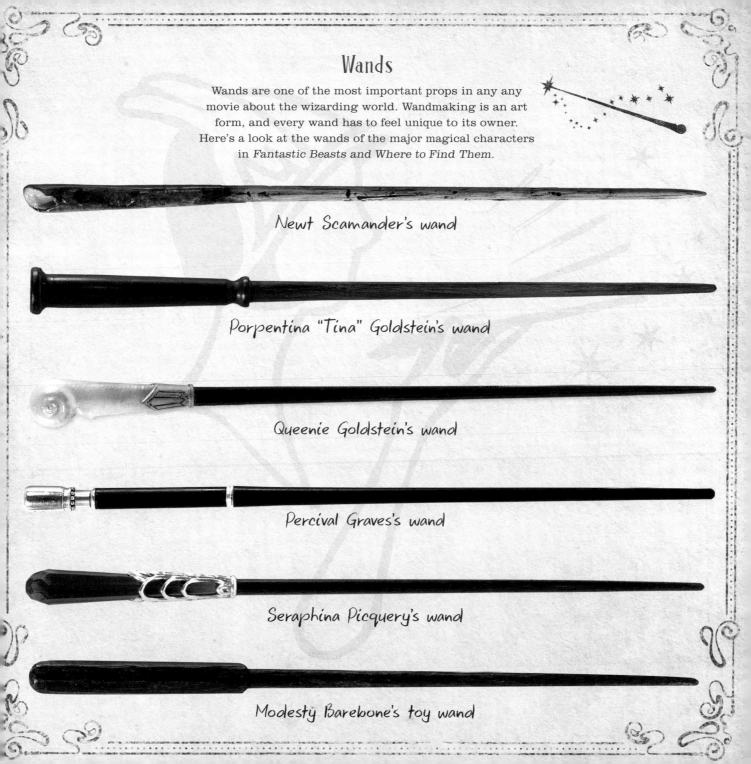

Newt Scamander's wand

Porpentina "Tina" Goldstein's wand

Queenie Goldstein's wand

Percival Graves's wand

Seraphina Picquery's wand

Modesty Barebone's toy wand

CREATURES

CREATING FANTASTIC BEASTS

$\mathcal{O}$ne of the highlights of *Fantastic Beasts and Where to Find Them* is, of course, Newt's interaction with his creatures. Newt's great love for them is part of the heart of the story—whether they're big or small, shy or aggressive, playful or dangerous (or both). Since these creatures are magical, the film's production team had to tackle the task of bringing them to life on the screen and making them feel believable.

The designers took their cues from Mother Nature. As visual effects supervisor Christian Manz puts it, "Nature in itself is pretty amazing!" In looking at photographs of the natural world, the team found that real-world creatures were often just as astonishing as any fantastic beast. "Reality can be more incredible than fantasy," explains producer David Heyman. "We're trying to root these a little more in nature and think about where these creatures could have come from."

Creature Categories

Much like real-world animals, the fantastic beasts of the wizarding world are classified in various ways. This chart designed for the film outlines the classification system, ranging from "known wizard killer" to "boring."

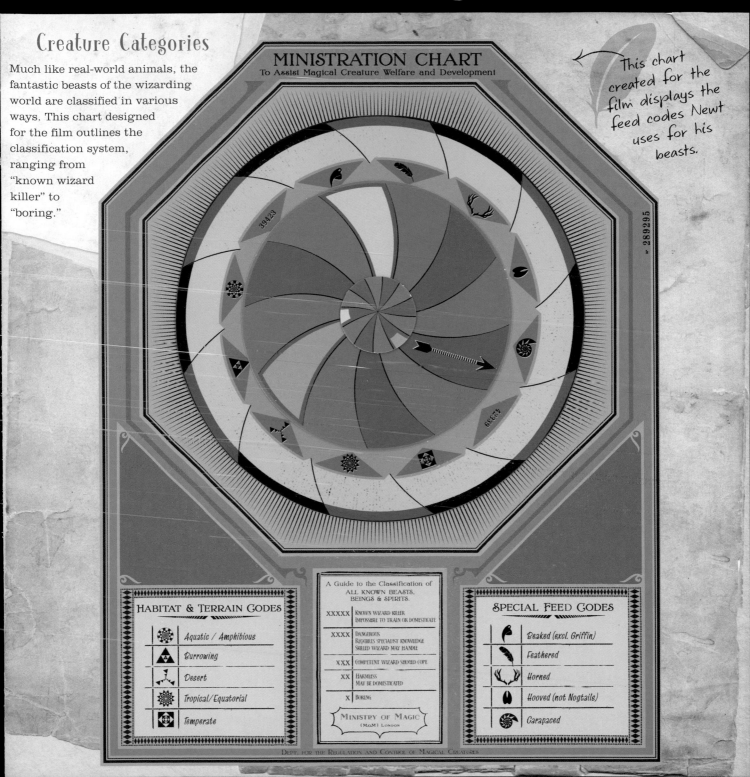

MINISTRATION CHART
To Assist Magical Creature Welfare and Development

This chart created for the film displays the feed codes Newt uses for his beasts.

" 289295

HABITAT & TERRAIN CODES

	Aquatic / Amphibious
	Burrowing
	Desert
	Tropical/Equatorial
	Temperate

A Guide to the Classification of ALL KNOWN BEASTS, BEINGS & SPIRITS.

XXXXX	KNOWN WIZARD KILLER IMPOSSIBLE TO TRAIN OR DOMESTICATE
XXXX	DANGEROUS REQUIRES SPECIALIST KNOWLEDGE SKILLED WIZARD MAY HANDLE
XXX	COMPETENT WIZARD SHOULD COPE
XX	HARMLESS MAY BE DOMESTICATED
X	BORING

MINISTRY OF MAGIC
(MoM) LONDON

SPECIAL FEED CODES

	Beaked (excl. Griffin)
	Feathered
	Horned
	Hooved (not Nogtails)
	Carapaced

DEPT. FOR THE REGULATION AND CONTROL OF MAGICAL CREATURES

NIFFLER

CLASSIFICATION: XXX

Newt's Niffler is definitely a star of the film. These gentle creatures have affectionate dispositions, but they find shiny objects quite irresistible and will do almost anything to acquire them. The Niffler bears a resemblance to a real-world mole. The snout depicted in this early image is similar to that of a platypus.

There are a *lot* of magical creatures in *Fantastic Beasts and Where to Find Them*. Putting so many amazing creatures into one movie posed a real challenge. In the end, computer animation brought them all to life, but each started as a piece of art. Elements of the natural world and the extraordinary traits of each creature can be seen in these initial illustrations.

Demiguise

CLASSIFICATION: XXXX

Another featured beast in the movie, Dougal the Demiguise, is an apelike creature from the Far East with precognitive sight, meaning he can see things before they happen. Demiguises can also turn invisible.

ERUMPENT

CLASSIFICATION: XXXX

This huge beast can be found thundering across the African plains. In terms of appearance, it is similar to a rhinoceros. But unlike its real world counterpart, the Erumpent's long, sharp horn is filled with deadly exploding fluid. Thus it can penetrate any target, including stone and metal.

SWOOPING EVIL

CLASSIFICATION: UNKNOWN

The Swooping Evil is a large winged creature with vivid green spikes across its back and a radiant blue coloring on its underside.

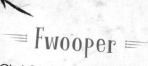

═ Fwooper ═

CLASSIFICATION: XXX

This small owl-like African bird features bright feathers of pink with hints of blue and green.

═ MURTLAP ═

CLASSIFICATION: XXX

The Murtlap is a small ratlike creature with a sprouting of tentacles that makes it look like it has a sea anemone on its back. The Murtlap's bite can be quite painful, as poor Jacob finds out the hard way in the film. As Dan puts it, "It's a hairless rat with tentacles. It's scary . . . and he bites me!"

MOONCALF

CLASSIFICATION: XX

This shy beast is aptly named, as it only emerges from its burrow during a full moon. In the film, Jacob feeds pellets to Newt's Mooncalf herd.

Bowtruckle

CLASSIFICATION: XX

These pixie-like tree guardians typically dwell in European forests, inhabiting trees used for wands. In the movie, Newt keeps a Bowtruckle named Pickett in his lapel and houses three others named Titus, Finn, and Jeremy in his sanctuary.

ᗌ Thunderbird ᗏ

CLASSIFICATION: UNKNOWN

This massive magical bird, native to the United States, can conjure up storms. Newt has come to the United States to release his Thunderbird, named Frank, back into its native environment.

BILLYWIG

CLASSIFICATION: XXX

This speedy Australian insect is sapphire blue. Its sting induces giddiness and levitation. Newt has a case of Billywig stingers in his shed.

Diricawl
CLASSIFICATION: XX

The fluffy-feathered Diricawl is a plump, flightless magical bird. Because of its teleportation ability, Muggles and No-Majs (who call it the "dodo") mistakenly believe the species is extinct.

DOXY
CLASSIFICATION: XXX

The Doxy is a small, sharp-toothed magical creature with beetle-like wings.

★ ★ ★ ★ ★ NEWT'S CASE ★ ★ ★ ★ ★

Creatures this extraordinary require a very special place to live. Newt keeps his beasts inside of his enchanted case, which not only gives each creature plenty of space to roam, but also re-creates their native habitats. Without a doubt, Newt's case is one of the most important props in the film—the story is set in motion after it is accidentally switched with Jacob's case.

While Newt's case might appear normal to the average No-Maj, looks can be deceiving. In addition to habitats, the case contains a shed full of supplies and souvenirs—and the characters themselves can all fit inside. To create the illusion of fully grown adults stepping into a case, the filmmakers created a set that was raised several feet off the ground. Then they placed a bottomless version of the case over a hole in the floor. This allowed Newt and Jacob to appear as though they were descending into the case.

A case of
Billywig
stings ←

BILLYWIG STINGS

Medicines
and
potions
stored
in Newt's
office ↘

Newt has
traveled far and
wide in his search
for magical
creatures.

Newt's Shed

The first room Newt and
Jacob enter after descending
into the case is Newt's shed,
which was decorated to resemble
a field zoologist's work space
from that era. An oasis for
Newt, it was filled with items
that relate to his interests, his
creatures, and his explorations.
Maps, pictures, and drawings fill
the walls, as do Newt's notes on
caring for his creatures.

Newt's Magical Habitats

Outside the shed is where Newt's creatures are kept—a kind of safari park the size of an aircraft hangar, full of magical habitats. The filmmakers thought hard about where each fantastic creature would live if they really existed: What would they need from their environments? What would their habitats look like? Would they be hot or cold? Tropical or desert-like? In the case of the Niffler, it was imagined that this coin-collecting creature would need a burrow to keep his loot safe. In the film, Newt's Niffler has a small patch of grass and a tree—a relatively simple space where he can burrow into the ground to hoard his shiny finds!

STREELER JACOB

JACOB

KAPPA

MOONCALVES

BOWTRUCKLE

JACOB

OCCAMY   NEWT

NIFFLER

An early layout of the set for Newt's creature habitats. It blocks out how Newt and Jacob move through the area.

Niffler habitat

Bowtruckle habitat

Thunderbird
habitat

WHAT'S NEXT?

Fantastic Beasts and Where to Find Them is a fantastic story—a rich, full meal, as it were. It has everything. But now we're all hungry for more, aren't we?

—DAVID YATES, DIRECTOR

Newt Scamander arrived in New York City as an outsider, both as a Brit in 1920s New York and as someone who cherishes dangerous, beautiful, and exotic magical beasts. "But he's also an outsider because he doesn't have any deep human connections," says director David Yates. By the end of the film, so much has changed. In his companions, Newt has found a great new cohort of friends—people who have come to share his love and affection for fantastic beasts. Together they have discovered some of the secrets of the wizarding world. But where will Newt go next?

First U.S. edition 2016

ISBN 978-0-7636-9590-3

Published by
Candlewick Press
99 Dover Street
Somerville, Massachusetts 02144
visit us at www.candlewick.com

Produced by

INSIGHT
EDITIONS
PO Box 3088
San Rafael, CA 94912
www.insighteditions.com

Publisher: Raoul Goff
Co-publisher: Michael Madden
Executive Editor: Vanessa Lopez
Art Director: Chrissy Kwasnik
Designer: Jenelle Wagner
Project Editor: Greg Solano
Production Editor: Rachel Anderson
Production Managers: Thomas Chung,
    Alix Nicholaeff, and Lina sp Temena
Production Coordinator: Leeana Diaz
Production Assistant: Sam Taylor

 REPLANTED PAPER

Insight Editions, in association with Roots of Peace, will
plant two trees for each tree used in the manufacturing
of this book. Roots of Peace is an internationally
renowned humanitarian organization dedicated to
eradicating land mines worldwide and converting war-
torn lands into productive farms and wildlife habitats.
Roots of Peace will plant two million fruit and nut trees
in Afghanistan and provide farmers there with the skills
and support necessary for sustainable land use.

Manufactured in Shaoguan, Guangdong, China,
by Insight Editions

20165903R0
16 17 18 19 20 21 SFC 10 9 8 7 6 5 4 3 2 1